Don't Eat That!

The Absolutely True Story of Buzz

Written by Debbie Witmer

Illustrated by Lesian S.

I am sooooooooo bored.
Bored and lonely.

Hi Buzz!

Bandit!
Bandit!
Bandit!

Yikes!

Buzz, are you okay?
Whoa...

I think my nose fell off.
No. It’s still there.

But really Buzz...
Are you okay?
I okay. Why you
call me that?

Because your name is Buzz.
No, it's not!
Yes it is.
Not!

Buzz is a great name. You should be proud of your name.
Hmmph. I no look at you.

Don't be mad. If Buzz isn't your name then what is it?

My name is
Don't.Eat.That!

Why do you think your name is Don't Eat That?

You're saying it wrong. You gotta say it real fast and all together. Don't.Eat.That!

Why do you think your name is Don't. Eat. That!
My people call me that. All. The. Time.

They call me Don’t. Eat. That! last night.
And what were you doing?

New Shoes

Well they call me Don't. Eat. That! again this morning too.
What were you doing then?

New
Underwear

Shoes! Underwear! Was there anything else?

Garbage

You're silly.
Let's go outside.

Maybe if you stopped eating stuff they would call you Buzz again.
I duno. Maybe.

I don't care what they call you. You're my best pal!

Tastes like chicken...
Ribbit.
Don't. Eat. That!

See. I told you that's my name.